Art Collecting for Profit

An Alternative Route to Wealth-Building

Table of Contents

Chapter 1. Introduction

Unveiling the mesmerizing world of fine art, our Special Report, "Art Collecting for Profit: An Alternative Route to Wealth-Building," transports you into a realm where beauty and finance dance a fascinating duet. This report is not just for the aesthetics enthusiast, but also for the ingenious investor looking to diversify and solidify their wealth portfolio. It imparts a fresh perspective on investment, one that strays from the conventional norms, igniting an unprecedented joy that enriches your soul and your pockets. Doubt not, the allure of the canvas and the allure of capital are far from mutually exclusive. Ready yourself to embark on an enticing path where appreciation of beauty becomes a strategy for success. Just one paragraph in, and you're already on the brink of a new adventure. Order this Special Report today to unravel the connection between your love for art and the art of wealth-building!

Chapter 2. Understanding the Basics of Art Collecting

Art collecting, a vocation that has been practiced by individuals with devotion and passion, dates back several centuries. A nuanced venture that is filled with allure, intrigue, and sophistication, it requires deeper understanding of various elements to truly appreciate, evaluate, and strategically invest in.

2.1. The Origins of Art Collecting

Starting on your journey into art collection, it's crucial to understand why it has been a popular activity for a long time. The act of art collecting began with the princely courts of Europe during the Renaissance. Royalty and nobility made significant efforts to amass works of art, assembling collections that were both a testament to their wealth and status, but also a sign of cultural sophistication. But it's not simply a historical phenomenon, even today, art collecting continues to play a crucial role in shaping societal and cultural narratives, projecting personal frame of reference, expression, and prestige, and most importantly in our context, building profitable investment dynamics.

2.2. Understanding Art as an Asset

Art collectors today make purchases not merely out of love for art, but they also understand its value as an appreciating asset. While great profit is not always sure-fire, art investments have time and again proven second to none. Just as a real estate asset, rare gemstone, or stocks, art offers a tangible security with unmeasured and limitless potential for appreciation.

2.3. The Appeal of Diverse Art Forms

One can collect a wide array of art forms, traditional or innovative, each holding its unique value and charm. Painting, the most common form, enjoys a variety of styles – from abstract, to surreal, to contemporary, and impressionist. However, collections aren't exclusively limited to paintings. Photography, sculpture, installations, digital art, and even video art have found their righteous place in both domestic and international art markets. Exploring these diverse forms can broaden your horizons and deepen your appreciation for art, while strategically diversifying your investment portfolio.

2.4. Learning About Artists and Art Periods

Being an informed art collector involves knowing the key players: the artists. Building an understanding of various artists' oeuvres, the periods or movements they belong to, their historic and cultural contexts, can significantly improve your discernment as a collector. Knowing if an artist is established, emerging, or overlooked can often help predict the future value of their work. Similarly, knowledge of art periods or movements can inform a collector which art style might be due for a resurgence in popularity.

2.5. Grasping the Art Market

The art market is driven by various elements - fluctuating global economies, trends, tastes, and sentiments. It requires meticulous observation and detail-oriented analysis. The primary market, where artworks are bought directly from artists or galleries, offers opportunities to discover emerging names. The secondary market, including auction houses, is typically where established artists' works are traded, sometimes for astronomical sums. However, make no mistake, the art market exhibits mercurial tendencies and is not immune to global crises or pressures. Therefore, successful navigation warrants careful vigilance and foresight.

2.6. Evaluating Art

When purchasing art with a view to seeing it appreciate, evaluation becomes critical. This involves a series of considerations like - the artist's contribution, reputation, professional trajectory, the artwork's originality, condition, provenance, and visibility in the market. The significance of these factors may vary from work to work, but in essence, these comprise the primary metrics for evaluation.

2.7. Building and Caring for Your Collection

Starting a collection can seem intimidating, but it's important to remember that it's a personal journey. It's essential to choose works that resonate with you as a collector. Once you have started acquiring pieces, you should ensure proper conservation. Majority of the artworks are delicate, undergoing environmental wear and tear. Hence, they need proper care, right from handling and framing to storage and exhibition.

2.8. Engaging with the Art Community

Finally, be an active participant in the art community. Attend gallery openings, biennials, art fairs, auctions, and symposia. Engage in discussions, network with other collectors, artists, dealers, and auctioneers. This will not only enrich your understanding but also create windows of opportunities for better deals or even allow you access to early works of an emerging artist before they hit mainstream.

Art collecting is a thrilling journey of discovery, but it's also an exercise in patience, discernment, and strategy. Like any investment, it comes with its risks, but armed with information and a keen eye, you stand to not only survive, but thrive, in this unique marketplace.

Chapter 3. The Intersection of Passion and Profit

Perhaps the most intriguing question for the art collector and the financier alike is how these two distinct interests intersect. The lines are often blurred and the interplay can be captivating, making the world of investing in fine art all the more compelling. Here's how passion and profit come together in the realm of art.

3.1. The Quintessence of Art Investment

Art, as we understand it, is a form of emotional experience. It has the power to elicit potent emotions, stir dialogue, and move us in unexpected ways. Yet for the astute collector, art is also an asset – a tangible, valuable asset that can diversify a portfolio and potentially yield a significant return on investment.

Investing in art is an uncommon but sagacious move. Unlike traditional investments like stocks and bonds, art purchases are not tied to the performance of the stock market. This inherent independence makes art a distinct route to wealth-building, insulated from the financial meltdowns that often ravage wall street. While its value may fluctuate due to market demands, it generally tends to appreciate over time.

3.2. On the Emotional Appreciation of Art

Art collection is not for the faint-hearted. The complexity of the market, the nebulous nature of art "value," the difficulty of assessing provenance and authenticity, and the sheer amount of time and knowledge required to understand and navigate this distinctive world are significant barriers. Yet for those who possess a real joy for art, the journey is part of the appeal.

The emotional appreciation of art may inspire more informed purchase decisions. A deep love for and understanding of art may lead to wise acquisitions that are intuitively aligned with emerging trends. When you buy art that you love, you're investing in your personal joy and well-being, which remains invaluable no matter the current market value of the piece.

3.3. The Mechanics of Art as an Investment

Art as an investment operates a bit differently than other forms of investment. Here, you're investing in something tangible, unique, and irreplaceable. But how exactly does it work?

Upon purchase, an artwork becomes part of your asset base. With the right acumen and strategy, that asset may then be sold in the future at an appreciably higher price. While it's an attractive concept, in practicality, it requires deep understanding of artists, genres, provenance, condition, rarity, and factors influencing value.

Navigating the art world's subtleties requires expertise and experience. One must follow auction results, market trends, and artistic movements, and have discerning disciplines that guide their buying decisions. It's this rigorous process that unravels the real meaning of investing in art.

3.4. The Role of Art Advisors

Where does one begin on this journey? Just as in traditional investing, professional advice can be invaluable. Expert art advisors can inform you about what to buy, when to buy, and the price to pay.

They can help you build a coherent collection that balances personal satisfaction with potential financial gain.

Art advisors act like your very own art brokers. They're equipped with the gobsmacking knowledge of the art world, have contacts with artists and galleries, and understand the intricacies of the market. They're able to guide you through the labyrinth of the artmarket, ensuring you steer clear of forgery and financial pitfalls. When choosing an art advisor, it's paramount to consider their reputation, knowledge level, and their alignment to your investment objectives and aesthetic preferences.

3.5. The Long-Term Nature of Art Investing

Consider art investing as a long game, not a quick-play. While there may be instances when art skyrocketed overnight due to sporadic trends, the reality is that most art worth investing in appreciates over time.

It's often the works that resonate with you on a deeply emotional level that will also find favor in the market years later. The trick is to find the confluence of your personal taste and what other collectors and institutions might find desirable. Hence backing contemporary artists who are still alive and producing work can be a better strategy than shooting for old masters – a segment that's becoming increasingly rare and expensive, and at the same time, often fraught with issues of provenance and authenticity.

3.6. Conclusion: A Balanced Approach

The key to successful art investing often stands on the fine balance between personal aesthetic fulfillment and potential financial gain.

Indeed, the intersection of passion and profit is where the true magic of art as an investment comes alive. By acquiring art that moves you, while strategically considering its place in the market, you stand the chance to not just grow your wealth but also enrich your life in an immeasurable sense. Pursue your artistic passion with an astute mind for financial gain, and the path to profit through the world of art may well be laid before you.

Remember that venturing into art collecting is not merely a commercial endeavor, but, importantly, an enriching human experience. The journey through galleries, meeting artists, cataloging your collection and seeing it appreciated by visitors and critics alike – all these elements contribute to an emotional payoff that enriches the experience beyond the financial.

While the path of art investment may seem daunting at first, the integration of interest, knowledge, and careful financial strategies have the potential to turn art into a remarkable investment. The joy and satisfaction of owning a beautiful piece of art that you love coupled with the anticipation of its potential future value creates the perfect intersection of passion and profit.

Chapter 4. The Art Market: A Primer

Despite its elegant and dramatic nature, the art market is, arguably, a gray zone replete with nuances that could feel labyrinthian for the uninitified. Here, we will provide you an exhaustive deep dive into this lustrous sphere, helping you familiarize with the art world's fluid ebb and flow.

4.1. The Structure of the Art Market

The structure of the art market can be understood most succinctly by separating it into two distinct realms: the primary and secondary markets.

The primary market refers to the sale of artworks for the first time, typically through a gallery or an artist's representative. This segment is dynamic and often predicated on the artist's reputation, demand for their work, and the desire for novelty among collectors.

The secondary market, on the other hand, deals with the sale of artworks that have previously been purchased or are 'second hand.' These transactions transpire at auction houses, online platforms, and sometimes even galleries. The prices here are driven by provenance, rarity, condition, among other factors. Artworks by deceased artists exclusively trade in the secondary market.

4.2. Channels of Art Trade

Besides galleries and auctions, various other conduits play crucial roles in this economically significant landscape. These include art fairs, online platforms, private dealers, and even direct transactions between collectors.

Art fairs, comprising a variety of galleries, have emerged as a major source of plentiful sales, allowing artists, collectors, and curators to converge. South Florida's Art Basel and New York's Frieze are prime exemplars of such marquee events.

Online platforms, venerable in recent years, essentially break geographical barriers and timelines, bringing art collecting to the fingertips.

Private dealers and advisors, endowed with specialized knowledge, assist collectors through their extensive networks, accessing works not openly available on sale.

4.3. Economic Driving Forces of the Art Market

The motor behind the art market's economic might are high net worth individuals and institutional investors seeking to diversify their portfolios. Besides financial reasons, the appeal of owning and displaying exquisite artworks, the desire to support artists and cultural institutions, and sometimes even social prestige, stimulate the ever-increasing flow of capital in this sphere.

Developing countries' newly minted billionaires have become a major force, their involvement sparking significant shifts in the market. The flourishing Asian market, especially China, encapsulates this trend acutely.

4.4. Collecting Art and Building Wealth

Notwithstanding its appeal, art is not a guaranteed profit-making venture. Historical data reveals art investments yield mixed returns, cautioning each investor to conduct due diligence.

The rewards of art investment hinge on a tapestry of factors: the artist's established reputation, the piece's proven condition, its historical significance, market trends, geopolitics, and of course, an element of luck.

A conscientious collector learns to balance the desire for beauty with the understanding that not all art acquisitions will appreciate significantly. They intrinsically find joy in the works they own, even as they aim for sound financial performance.

4.5. The Auction Market and Its Mechanics

Auctions are perhaps the most theatrical component of the art market. Here the curtain is raised on the raw clash of demand and supply. Auction houses like Sotheby's, Christie's, and Phillips are the anchoring establishments of the global auction industry.

The auction process begins with the consignment of a work for sale. It is evaluated, authenticated, and appraised before being listed in the auction catalogue alongside an estimate. The climax ensues on the auction day, where fevered bidding can catapult the hammer price to record-breaking heights, much beyond the estimate.

It's important to note that auctions aren't just stages for antique masterpieces. They play a vital role in determining the market value of contemporary artists as well, influencing valuations even in the primary market.

4.6. Future Trends

Technology's advent has been disruptive for the art market, mirroring its impact across industries. Blockchain, AI, and VR technologies have begun to stir the waters.

Blockchain's transparent and immutable ledger system breathes trust into art transactions, heightening security, and authenticity. AI art, on the other hand, provokes fundamental questions about the nature of creativity, even as AI-assisted curation caters to individual preferences, maximizing sales.

Virtual Reality enables virtual globetrotting, transforming the experience of art browsing into an immersive journey unrestricted by spatial constraints.

Whether or not these trends revolutionize the art market or merely become moderating forces, they surely signal towards exciting days ahead.

Endeavoring to capitalize on the art market requires careful navigation, meticulous research, and a judicious blend of passion and pragmatism. An art piece that catches the eye should also be subjected to a fiscally discerning gaze. By investing in this primer guide, you've already taken the first step towards mastering the sophisticated interplay between aesthetics and economics that personifies the art market. Now, gear up to delve further, decoding more complex layers of this fascinating world.

Chapter 5. The Role of Auction Houses and Galleries in Art Trading

In any discourse about art trading, auctions and galleries dutifully take center stage as the prevailing actors in this muse-infused financial theater. They enact the crucial roles of enhancing visibility for artists, styling the trajectory of art style trends, and, most importantly, facilitating the buying and selling of artworks.

5.1. Auction Houses: Understanding their Function

Auction houses, with their historical root traced to the commoditized art scene of 17th-century Europe, have morphed into influential powerhouses in the contemporary art market. Today, they stand as unshakeable pillars of the high-end art market, servicing both established and aspiring art collectors through public and sometimes, private auctions.

At an auction, a wide array of artworks spanning various styles, epochs, and price points are up for grab. Auction houses bank on the bespoke thrill of live bidding, which arguably adds an electrifying layer to art acquisition.

Not merely a marketplace, auction houses ubiquitously contribute towards setting art market trends and values. They apprehend the pulse of the demand and supply in the art ecosystem, helping shape the perceived worth of artworks. This pricing function of auction houses cannot be overlooked, as they dynamically influence the trajectory of an artist's reputation and market value.

5.2. The Mechanics of Auction Houses

Auctioning of an artwork is no arbitrary affair. It is a meticulous process, meticulously planned and executed over months. First off, the auction house must take possession of an artwork, which often comes from private collectors, estates, or directly from artists. The artwork then undergoes rigorous appraisal to assure its authenticity and condition, and to form an estimate of its market value.

Once the artwork is cataloged and the value estimate completed, it is listed in the auction house's catalogue - a key point of reference for potential buyers. It offers vital information about the artwork such as its provenance, artist's details, and expected price range.

The climax of this process entails the live auction event. Interested buyers compete in an open forum, placing bid against bid, each attempt escalating until only the highest bidder remains standing. This transparent competitiveness means artworks often fetch prices beyond their listed estimates, and at times, shatter previous records.

5.3. The Powerhouses of Auctions

The global art auction market is dominated by renowned names such as Christie's and Sotheby's, who have purveyed artworks to wealthy connoisseurs for centuries. But they're not alone. Scores of regional, national and international auction houses, like Bonhams, Phillips, and Dorotheum, function dexterously within niche markets, catering to diverse collector preferences.

These firms play an important role in incubating interest among new collectors, by selling artworks at a more accessible price range. Their influence on the art market and its dynamics cannot be overstated. They often dictate the direction the market will take, based on the works they source and the sales they promote.

5.4. Galleries: The More Personalised Affair

Meanwhile, galleries offer a more personalized, intimate platform for art trading. Functioning as intermediaries, they represent a selected roster of artists and strive to sell their works to potential collectors.

Galleries play a crucial role in building an artist's career, assisting in their professional development and managing their reputations. They stimulate demand for an artist's work, which eventually elevates their market value. Through curated exhibitions, strategic pricing, and astute networking, galleries help shape the perception of artists, defining the supply and demand mechanics of their works.

5.5. How Galleries Work

Brimming with curated art displays, galleries are both a sanctuary for the aesthetics enthusiast and a marketplace for the investor. Unlike the electrifying ambiance of auctions, galleries provide a markedly tranquil setting, allowing potential buyers to leisurely engage with the artworks.

When a collector purchases from a gallery, they're often building a relationship directly with the gallerist and, by extension, the artist. This intimate experience can add an extra dimension to the ownership of the art, amplifying its sentimental and potential future monetary value.

Galleries focus on nurturing relationships with buyers. This often involves introducing buyers to new artists, advising them on current trends, and ultimately guiding them in making purchases that will appreciate over time.

5.6. The Influential Galleries

The gallery landscape teems with influential entities, each carving out a niche within the art ecosystem. Power galleries like Gagosian, David Zwirner and Hauser & Wirth frequently feature works from established artists and command significant pricing power. Smaller galleries, on the other hand, often represent emerging artists providing a valuable foothold for up-and-coming talent in the tough terrain of the art market.

5.7. The Interplay Between Auction Houses and Galleries

Despite navigating the same art arena, the modus operandi of auction houses and galleries is distinct, yet they often intersect and complement each other.

An artist's value can be significantly impacted by the price their work fetches at auction, and successful auctions can often generate interest in an artist's other works, which are often sold at galleries. When a new record is set at an auction, it can drive up prices for that artist's work across the board, reinforcing the gallery's position. Conversely, if an artwork fails to sell or sells for less at an auction, it could hamper the artist's market value.

Hence, the dance between auction houses and galleries is a captivating duet - a dance of inter-dependence where one's step influences the other's direction. Together, they shape the dynamic, complex, and utterly fascinating world of art trading.

In conclusion, auction houses and galleries are not just mere venues for buying and selling art. They are integral components of the art-market machinery, each contributing indispensably to the ebb and flow of the broader art investing spectrum. It is crucial for the savvy art investor to comprehend their role and influence while embarking on the prosperous path of art collecting.

Chapter 6. Strategies for Building a Profitable Art Collection

Understanding the fine art world is an adventure in itself, akin to trekking through uncharted digital landscapes, exploring the mysteries of a timeless painting, or decrypting an abstract sculpture. Building a profitable art collection isn't solely about choosing pieces you adore; it's also about understanding the landscape and adopting effective strategies for success. As we journey through the process, you'll discover how to identify opportunities, balance risk versus reward, and craft a collection that brings you both pleasure and profit.

6.1. Art as an Investment

Fine art is a unique and tantalizing asset class that has piqued the interest of many investors worldwide. Unlike traditional investments like stocks or real estate, fine art allows alternative wealth-building across diversified realms. It has a low correlation with other asset types, making it an effective hedge against market volatility.

However, art investing entails risks and challenges that are different from conventional investment channels. Understanding these will help you better navigate this unique landscape. Remember, the value and price of art are highly subjective and influenced by various factors such as the artist's reputation, the era or style of the artwork, its condition, historical significance, and market supply-demand dynamics.

For an art collection to remain profitable, its growth should outperform inflation rates. Therefore, always gauge the potential return against associated risks. This is where research and expert advice come indispensable.

6.2. Building Your Art Knowledge

A profitable art collection begins with a firm understanding of the art world, its dynamics, trends, and players. Just as an investor wouldn't put money into stocks without understanding the stock market, you shouldn't invest in art without studying the field. Dedicate time to learning about different art styles, periods, and movements. Study auction catalogs and visit art fairs, galleries, and museums. Engage in conversations with artists, dealers, and other collectors to broaden your understanding and network.

Starting small can also be an excellent learning strategy. Invest in less-expensive artworks by emerging artists. These purchases will allow you to learn from experience without the risk of significant financial loss.

6.3. Defining Your Art Collection Strategy

Identify a collecting strategy that aligns with your passion, your knowledge, and your investment strategy. Some collectors focus on specific eras or movements, while others accumulate works from a diverse range of artists and styles. Both approaches can be lucrative, but a focused collection often has a more stable value and is typically easier to manage.

6.4. Leveraging Expert Insights and Networks

Rely on the expertise of those with established market knowledge. This includes auctioneers, art agents, consultants, and galleries. Seek their advice on purchasing decisions to increase your chances of acquiring profitable pieces. These experts can alert you to hidden gems and price anomalies and help you avoid falling into costly traps or buying forgeries.

6.5. Investment Metrics: Tracking Performance

This strategy targets artworks that show strong potential for appreciation based on historical performance data. Many platforms provide comprehensive art market analysis and statistics that collectors can tap into. By comparing prices at auction and tracking historical growth trends, you can identify promising opportunities and forecast possible returns.

However, note that past performance is not a sole guarantee of future value. Therefore, refrain from relying solely on metrics and allow room for instinct and passion.

6.6. Exploring Emerging Global Markets

With a keen eye and open mind, explore art from emerging markets worldwide. It's often possible to find significant value in these areas, as contemporary artists from under-explored regions have massive growth potential. However, be wary of the potential risks involved, including ensuring authenticity, understanding cultural variations, and navigating logistical issues like shipping and import duties.

6.7. Balancing Emotion and Economics

It is crucial to balance the love for aesthetics with economic considerations. While an artwork's beauty and emotional resonance might endear it to you, these factors may not convert into financial value. Always evaluate art considering both its intrinsic aesthetic appeal and its potential to appreciate monetarily.

6.8. Care and Conservation

Being a good steward of the works in your collection is as crucial as picking them right. This means preserving the artwork in a way that maintains its condition and protects its value. From proper display and storage to the use of conservation professionals, care and conservation are crucial elements in preserving the monetary value and aesthetic integrity of your collection.

By combining a strong understanding of the art market with coherent investment strategies, you can create an art collection that not only resonates on a personal level but also serves as a powerful wealth-building tool. Above all, remember to enjoy the thrill of discovery and the pleasure of ownership - after all, you're not just collecting art, you're also amassing life-defining experiences and tales.

Chapter 7. Emerging Artists versus Established Masters: Where to Invest?

Art collecting is classified into two main categories — purchasing works from emerging artists or investing in pieces created by established masters. Both these avenues hold unique allure and present individualistic opportunities and risks. This chapter will dissect the pros and cons of investing in both categories highlighting their particular intricacies, thus assisting you in astute decision-making.

7.1. The Allure of Emerging Artists

Investing in emerging artists holds its unique charm. It allows you to discover talent at the infancy of its full blossoming, enabling you to hold a piece of history in the making. Buying pieces from emerging artists also speaks volumes about our vision and risk appetite as a collector.

The principal advantage here lies in the attractive pricing of artworks by the emerging talent. A carefully chosen piece might cost significantly less than that of an established artist. This opens doors to an affordable entry into the world of art collecting, hence, broadening the investor base.

However, one has to note that lesser-known artists are not devoid of risks. Art is subjective, and public reception could vary tremendously. Hence, while some artists might achieve stardom in a matter of a few years, others might never break out of their shell.

Another significant risk is the absence of a secondary market. Often, art pieces from emerging artists have less demand in resale markets, which can lead to difficulties in liquidating your investments.

7.2. Navigating Established Masters

Investing in established masters is the more traditional path within the art-investment community. Artworks from well-recognized artists are often perceived as 'blue-chip' investments that are likely to hold and potentially increase in value over time.

These pieces, having proven their artistry and retained their worth over time, often come with a hefty price tag. Still, they also bring along the reputation of the artist and a virtually guaranteed demand in the secondary market.

An experienced art collector or investor can benefit from the relatively predictable market patterns and trends for these artists. However, it's crucial to understand that these pieces, while largely stable, are not entirely insulated from market fluctuations.

A risk associated with established masterpieces is the high entry cost. Not every investor can afford the substantial upfront investment required, hence limiting the potential investor pool. Besides, the return on such investments often requires a significant time horizon and is not ideal for those seeking quick profits.

7.3. Portfolio Diversification: A Balanced Approach

Balancing the investment between emerging artists and established masters can be an optimal strategy for many. This approach allows for diversification, mitigating some of the risks involved in art investment.

Investing in emerging artists can provide potentially high returns, while established masters often promise more stability. A well-diversified portfolio may allow the investor to balance both risk and reward effectively.

7.4. Decision-Making Framework

When deciding where to invest, several factors come into play. These could be personal, like your risk appetite and liquidity need, or market-related, like art trends and economic conditions.

One of the key elements is understanding and appreciating the artist's work. Whether emerging or established, it's crucial to connect with the piece you are considering. Art investment should always foster a sense of pleasure and satisfaction.

Consider gaining insights into the artist's background, inspiration, and influence in the art community. Combining this understanding with market trends and conditions can result in a well-informed decision.

In essence, when deciding between investing in emerging artists or established masters, there isn't a universally correct choice. It greatly depends on individual risk tolerance, affordability, liquidity needs, and personal aesthetic appreciation. A wise art investor weaves a story with their art holdings, where each piece has its place and purpose. The key is to find a balance that works best for you, ensuring a beautiful portfolio that brings as much joy as it provides financial reward.

Chapter 8. The Significance of Art Authentication and Appraisal

Art authentication and appraisal hold significant value in the realm of art collection for profit. Collectors, whether seasoned or budding, need to run a two-fold process of proving a piece's genuineness and then determining its monetary value. This chapter delves deeply into these complementary and essential exercises to guide you in reaping the full benefits of art investment.

8.1. UNDERSTANDING ART AUTHENTICATION

Authentication could well be called the very foundation of art connoisseurship. This process verifies the artwork's history, dating it correctly, and establishing its authorship, thereby maintaining the integrity of the art world. It requires in-depth study, calling for expertise in art history and the application of multiple techniques of analysis to confirm a work's authenticity.

Art authentication aims to eliminate the risk of counterfeit artworks, which are a severe menace to the art market. Over time, forgeries have become more sophisticated, putting both novice and experienced collectors at potential risk. Understanding and effectively applying the art authentication process protects one's investment and maintains healthy market trust in the art collector community.

8.2. THE ART OF DISCERNING

The process of authentication often starts with connoisseurship or 'eye authentication.' These connoisseur skills are, essentially, a sophisticated understanding of the artist's style, methodology, materials, and contexts. One has to meticulously observe various fragments of the artwork – the brushwork, the color palette, the nature of the subject, amongst others.

A connoisseur will refer to catalogs raisonné, a comprehensive register of artworks by an artist, that sometimes include minutiae like sketches and workshop replicas, to compare the subject of investigation. Mastery in connoisseurship, while time-consuming to acquire, is an irreplaceable tool for any art investor.

8.3. SCIENTIFIC AUTHENTICATION

While connoisseur judgments are valuable, they are subjective and carry a margin of error. This is where scientific authentication comes into play. Scientific authentication, requiring material-technical expertise, provides objective judgments of the artwork. Techniques include the analysis of pigments, binders, fibers, and other materials which provide valuable information about the work's origin. These can range from infra-red reflectography to UV fluorescence.

For example, Carbon-14 testing could be used to determine the age of organic materials like wood or canvas, while thermoluminescence could date ceramics or stones. Knowing the probable age of materials helps discern the timeframe during which an artwork could have been created, assisting in authenticating it. Radiography and infra-red reflectography can reveal underdrawings and changes the artist might have made during the painting process – crucial clues in deducing if the painting is authentic.

8.4. PROVENANCE RESEARCH

Provenance is the history of the ownership of a work of art. It encompasses all known previous sales, collections held, exhibitions the artwork was included in, and relevant info like catalog entries. It is as much a part of the authentication process, providing a historical context and traceable lineage. While a strong provenance may enhance an artwork's credibility and value, it is not always definitive proof of authenticity.

There have been cases where provenance was fabricated, so the chain of ownership should be examined meticulously. Collectors should be aware that provenance contributes to authentication but on its own, can lead to a false sense of security.

8.5. THE ROLE OF ART APPRAISAL

Concurrent to art authentication is the art appraisal process. This is the practice of determining an artwork's market value or how much an item would most likely sell for on the open market. It is a dynamic practice that changes with trends, market shifts, and the general climate of the art world.

8.6. FACTORS THAT AFFECT APPRAISAL

The value attributed to a piece of art could be influenced by a plethora of factors. Provenance, condition, and rarity of the piece are significant influencers. The reputation of the artist also plays a vital role in assessing the artwork's value. Pieces from renowned artists (alive or deceased) fetch high prices in the market compared to lesser-known artists. The size of the artwork can impact its value. Larger artworks typically demand higher prices.

It's not just the physical aspects of the piece that can impact its appraisal. External factors, like market demand, can significantly sway the appraisal value. High demand for a particular artist or style can increase prices while low demand can reduce them.

8.7. METHODS OF ART APPRAISAL

There are three predominant methods of art appraisal – the sales comparison approach, the cost approach, and the income approach. The sales comparison approach is the most favored for fine art and involves comparing the subject artwork to similar artworks that have recently sold.

The cost approach, often used for lesser-known artists, evaluates the expenses that went into creating the artwork. This could include the artist's labor, cost of materials, and studio costs.

The income approach, infrequently used for fine art, is based on the income generation potential of the artwork, such as licensing reproductions or public display charges.

8.8. CERTIFIED PROFESSIONAL APPRAISERS

Art appraisal takes not only a deep understanding of art and art markets but also an objective viewpoint. You can seek this expertise from independent art appraisers or appraisal companies. Certified professional appraisers adhere to the Uniform Standards of Professional Appraisal Practice (USPAP) and the code of ethics stipulated by an accredited appraisal organization they are part of. Providing an unbiased and competent valuation, professional appraisers protect the interests of both buyers and sellers in the art market.

This complex dance of art authentication and appraisal is long, nuanced, and essential. By understanding these processes and employing them adeptly, art collectors can add an extra layer of assurance and profitability to their portfolio. The world of art investments thrives on both the aesthetic and fiscal soundness of the acquisitions and these practices ensure just that.

Chapter 9. Managing Risks and Rewards in Art Investment

Investing in art can yield substantial rewards, but like any investment, it also carries inherent risks. Understanding these risks, and knowing how to manage them, is crucial to success. On the other side of the coin, recognising potential rewards is equally important in mapping out your investment strategy.

9.1. Understanding the Risk-Reward Spectrum

Art investment falls under the umbrella of alternative investments, alongside assets like commodities, real estate, and private equity. These investments are often characterized by high return potentials and equally high risks. The first step toward managing these risks and rewards is to understand their existence and potential impact on your investment portfolio.

One of the most prominent risks with art investment is market volatility. Unlike more traditional investments such as stocks, art does not generate income passively. Its value is principally tied to the ebbs and flows of market demand, the reputation of the artist, the quality and preservation of the artwork, among other factors.

In comparison, the potential for high returns is a driving factor. A well-selected piece can appreciate significantly over time. For instance, in 1962, the National Gallery of Art in Washington, D.C., purchased Leonardo da Vinci's "Ginevra de' Benci" for around $5 million. Today, the piece is valued at over $450 million, highlighting the potential for astronomical returns in the art market. Yet, such success stories, while inspiring, make up only a small fraction of the art market.

9.2. Liquidity and Pricing in Art Investments

Unlike shares in publicly-traded companies or government bonds, art is a speculative and illiquid investment; you might not be able to sell your art quickly or at a profit. In general, returns are earned when the artwork is sold, which might take years or even decades, depending on market forces and the reputation of the artist.

Pricing of art is another area that presents both potential reward and risk. It's subjective, and various factors like the artist's reputation, the condition of the piece, market demand, provenance, and aesthetic trends affect how much a buyer will pay.

9.3. Diversification: A Cushion Against Market Volatility

Spreading your investments across different forms of art from various periods and artists is a proven method of managing risks associated with art investment. This strategy, known as diversification, helps to mitigate potential losses if an individual work or a specific artist's works do not perform well in the marketplace.

9.4. Investment in Emerging Artists: A High-Risk, High-Reward Venture

Emerging artists offer an exciting opportunity for investors. On the one hand, investing in these artists allows for potentially high returns if the artist becomes respected and renowned. However, investing in emergent artists can also entail higher risks. Unlike established artists, there is no guarantee that their work will appreciate over time.

9.5. Art Funds: Spreading and Sharing the Risks

For those unable or unwilling to jump into art as a solo venture, art investment funds are vehicles that pool resources from several investors to purchase a variety of artworks. This strategy reaps benefits from diversification, spreading the risk while promising potential capital appreciation when the fund assets are sold.

9.6. Art as Part of a Well-Balanced Portfolio

While the allure of art investment is captivating, a prudent investor will always ensure it forms part of a well-balanced portfolio. By diversifying investments across stocks, bonds, real estate, and alternative assets like art, you'll reduce exposure to specific risks associated with individual asset classes.

9.7. Importance of Research and Professional Guidance

Finally, any discussion on risk management in art investment would be incomplete without mentioning the importance of research and professional advice. Understanding market trends, the significance of an artist and their work, and the practical aspects of acquiring, storing, and selling art are all important factors that can cushion you from possible pitfalls and guide you towards greater rewards.

Appreciating art is fundamental, but appreciating the dynamics of the art market is equally vital. Balancing between the two is where the investor might reap significant rewards as the art world continues to evolve. Art can definitely be a rewarding investment, in more ways than one. Not only can it appreciate in value, but it offers something that stocks, bonds, and commodities often don't: the sheer joy of owning a beautifully crafted piece. Whether it's the brush strokes of an up-and-coming contemporary artist or the mastery of an old master, investing can be as much about the heart as it is about the wallet. The trick is balancing between the two.

Remember, the world of art investment can be murky and complex, but with the right guidance and strategy, it can also be rewarding. Do your homework, understand your risk tolerance, and enjoy the ride—the captivating journey towards investing in the artwork of your dreams and the potential financial rewards that accompany it.

Chapter 10. Art and Portfolio Diversification: The Winning Combo

The convergence point of two strikingly diverse fields, fine art and investment, might seem far-flung at first glance. However, upon closer examination, it becomes clear that the appeal and rationale for mixing these two lie in one indispensable aspect of financial planning – diversification. Here, we explore how the world of fine art offers alternative routes to wealth-building and risk management, thus providing an intriguing blend for your investment portfolio.

10.1. The What and Why of Diversification

In simple terms, diversification is a risk management strategy that involves spreading investments across various financial instruments, industries, and other categories to avoid exposure to any single asset or risk. The motive behind diversification is maximization of return by investing in different areas that would each react differently to the same occurrence.

Investment in art, relatively immune to the volatile ups and downs of the stock market, offers an alluring alternative. Art serves as an inflation hedge and its value can significantly appreciate over time. A well-diversified portfolio containing art investments therefore can stabilize your financial performance by providing a cushion against market volatility.

10.2. Art as a Component of Diversified Portfolio

With the advent of technology and the democratization of art markets, investing in art has become more accessible to all. Furthermore, characterized by its low correlation to traditional asset classes such as stocks and bonds, art ensures that your overall portfolio risk is significantly reduced.

Historically, art markets have demonstrated a steadfast performance during times of economic downturn, offering a safe haven to investors. One such instance is the 2008 global financial crisis, when despite economic turmoil, the art world proved to be resilient.

10.3. Making the Leap: From Collector to Investor

The journey of art collection begins with an appreciation for aesthetics. As a collector, one may find pleasure in owning a visual testament to human creativity. Conversely, an investor sees potential capital appreciation. The trick, however, lies in successfully combining the two – the aesthetic pleasure of a collector and the economic rationale of an investor.

Understanding when, where, and what to buy or sell takes a considerable amount of time, skill, and research. Observing market trends, networking with artists, sellers, and other collectors, and studying art history are all invaluable to navigating the sea of art investment.

10.4. Valuation of Art: The Essential Criteria

Unlike a dividend-paying stock or real estate that brings in rental income, art is considered a non-yielding asset where the return on investment is realized only upon sale. Therefore, the valuation of an artwork becomes critical. Although valuation of art intrinsically subjective, the following factors often come into play: the name of the artist, provenance, the artwork's condition, rarity, size, and market trends.

10.5. Managing Risks in Art Investment

Despite its potential for high returns, art investment is not free of risks. Value appreciation is never a guarantee, and illiquidity can be an issue. Additionally, forgery and authenticity issues underline the need for due diligence. Professional advice from art advisors or auction houses can help navigate these challenges for both seasoned investors and those making their first foray into the art market.

10.6. Resale: Realizing Art Investment Returns

The real test of art as an investment comes when it's time to sell. The two primary sales channels for art are auctions and private sales, each with their pros and cons. While auctions offer the potential for substantial returns if the artwork sparks a bidding war, private sales can offer quicker and more predictable outcomes.

By blending your passion for art and astute investment strategies, you can tap into the vibrant world of art investment - a world lined with creativity, wealth generation, and portfolio stability. Whether as a collector, investor, or a blend of both, you may find that art's enduring value makes it a viable contender for portfolio diversification.

Chapter 11. Case Studies: Success Stories in Art Investing

Art investing has shed light on a multitude of success stories. Stories of investors who weathered risk, identified hidden gems, and saw profits gush from their discerning taste and insightful purchases. It provides convincing arguments that prove the symbiotic relationship between passion for art and the pursuit of profits.

11.1. The Tale of David Geffen

David Geffen, a name synonymously resonating with both the music industry and the art world, is an inspiration for potential art investors. Geffen, a college dropout who started his career in the mailroom of William Morris, turned entertainment mogul, whose net worth now totals an estimated $9.8 billion. But beyond his substantial success in the music world, Geffen's art portfolio stands as the emblem of his predominantly astute investment moves.

His collection, which once included works by Willem De Kooning and Jackson Pollock, was gradually invested in starting in the 70s and 80s. Moving forward to 2006, he sold Pollock's "No. 5, 1948" for a whopping $140 million. As if that weren't astonishing enough, in 2015, he sold two pieces—"Woman III" by De Kooning and "No. 17A" by Pollock—to hedge funder Ken Griffin for a mesmerizing $500 million. Now that's an astronomical return on investments you can't ignore.

11.2. Driven by Curiosity: Hyman Bloom

Unlike David Geffen, Hyman Bloom never saw himself as an investor but rather as a devoted and passionate art appreciator. Bloom emigrated in 1920 to the United States from Latvia, and his obsession with art began as a teenager in Boston. He carved a niche for himself as a visionary artist, and his work garnered the attention of the world in the mid-20th century.

However, the value of Bloom's paintings in the market dwindled with changing art world trends. When he passed away in 2009, his work had long fallen out of the limelight. However, their value started surging again ten years later, and today, Bloom's paintings sell for six-figure sums, representing significant returns for early collectors who believed in Bloom's talent, held on to their pieces, and patiently waited for the market to recognize his genius again.

11.3. Carlos Slim: An Art Collection Par Excellence

One of the wealthiest men in the world, Carlos Slim, is known for his heavy investments in the telecommunications sector. However, he has also nurtured a profound passion for art. Slim's father ignited this passion by gifting him a bond which sparked an interest in investment, and a Coin of Carlos III which aroused his interest in art. Since then, there was no looking back.

Slim purchased his first painting when he was just 26—a landscape by José María Velasco, known as the "father of Mexican landscape art." Slim's real success in art investment began when he started purchasing European Old Masters during Mexico's financial crisis in the 1980s, when such artwork was selling at extremely depressed prices. Today, Slim owns more than 66,000 pieces of fine art, including a significant number of European and Mexican works, which he displays in his Museo Soumaya in Mexico City, named after his late wife. His collection is valued at over a billion dollars now, highlighting the scale of wealth growth possible through art investment.

These case studies provide glimpses into the world of art investing, highlighting the significance of research, patience, perseverance, and a discerning eye for potential assets. While it may not follow the traditional paths of wealth accumulation, the inspirations it offers are indeed limitless. Art investing can be a daunting prospect initially, but as these success stories demonstrate, it can also become not only a viable but also an overwhelmingly profitable venture for those who dare to step outside their comfort zones. Over time, more investors are realizing that a newfound passion for art could carve out the path to substantial wealth accumulation they've been looking for all along.

www.ingramcontent.com/pod-product-compliance
Lightning Source LLC
Chambersburg PA
CBHW071012260726
48661CB00007B/2914